# When She Speaks

A collection of words and thoughts…Vol. 2

A collection of words and thoughts...Vol. 2

# Amber Whitted

Chicago

WHEN SHE SPEAKS: A COLLECTION OF WORDS AND THOUGHTS – VOLUME 2

Copyright © 2015 by Amber Whitted. All rights reserved. Printed in the United States of America. No part of this book may be reproduced in any manner whatsoever without permission except in the case of brief quotations embodied in critical articles or reviews. Day Blue Green Night books may be purchased for educational, business, or sales promotional use. For additional information, address Day Blue Green Night Publishing, P.O. Box 945, Dolton, IL. 60419-0945

www.eshewords.com

Cover artwork: Creative Blessings by Jelaine Bell, © 2015
Website: www.creativeblessingsdesign.com

Library of Congress Cataloging-in-Publication Data

Whitted, Amber, 1981 –
  – 1st ed p.cm
  ISBN-13: 978-0692-55209-4
  ISBN-10: 0-692-55209-X
    1. Poetry  2. Poetry – African American  3. African American Literature  I. Title

First edition: November 2015

10 9 8 7 6 5 4 3 2 1

# A Dedication

I was thinking about you –
nothing long-winded,
nothing deep,
nothing elaborate.
It was just a simple thought of you
that caused me to smile,
pick up my pen,
and write.

# Table of Contents

**What Remains To Be Said (An Introduction)**

**...The Soul Is Stirred**

| | |
|---|---|
| Declarations | 2 |
| Sista Solitude | 6 |
| A Recipe For Pound Cake | 7 |
| Upon Admiration | 8 |
| 'Nuff Said | 10 |
| Lady In Red | 12 |

**...Love Is Evident**

| | |
|---|---|
| Coffee Shop | 14 |
| Gentlemen | 16 |
| I Wasn't Trying To Love You | 18 |
| Daydreaming | 19 |
| Symbiosis | 20 |
| My Letter To Atlas | 22 |

**...Her People Are United**

| | |
|---|---|
| Cry | 24 |
| Jungles | 28 |
| Black Mother's Plea | 31 |
| The Call | 32 |
| Being Black | 37 |
| Celebration Of Brown | 38 |

**...The Truth Is Heard**

| | |
|---|---|
| White Girl | 42 |
| Bitter, Party Of One | 45 |
| A Eulogy For Beauty | 46 |

| | |
|---|---|
| Letter 628 | 49 |
| 10 Things I've Been Meaning To Say To Black Women | 50 |
| Beauty's Sonnet | 54 |

## …Her God Listens

| | |
|---|---|
| One Day At A Time | 56 |
| My Desire | 57 |
| The Weight | 58 |
| Every Word Spoken | 61 |
| God's Creation | 62 |
| Nothing | 63 |
| What More Can I Do | 64 |

# What Remains To Be Said...
Introduction / Acknowledgements

*Let the words of my mouth and the meditation of my heart be acceptable in your sight, O LORD, my rock and my redeemer.*
*(Psalm 19:14)*

Thank you, Father, for allowing me to have the gift of words and the chance to share them. I am grateful and humbled that You have chosen me. All glory and praise belong to You.

I remember being the little girl that wrote and sang about everything. I was the adorably loquacious child that took 20 minutes to describe an action that happened in 30 seconds (I still do that, by the way). I was unashamed to have thick glasses and a full head of hair. Yes, I was that child – the dreamer.

Then life happened. I was introduced to a world where you had to be aesthetically pleasing to be valued. Faith became fear, and failure became frequent. Tears were replaced by cynicism, so healing was no longer an option. I hid in the shadows of foes posed as friends and purposely dimmed my light. To add insult to injury, I became comfortable with it. I allowed myself to become an expert at lying so everyone believed that I was ok. I wasted opportunities and made excuses. I bought into the lie – hook, line, and sinker – and convinced myself that I didn't deserve to live, laugh, or love.

The funny thing about dreams is that they never die until we choose to kill them. On a Friday night in December 2013, I did something that I hadn't done in a long time – I attended an open mic. That night, I performed a piece entitled *Declarations*. And it felt good. A month later, I boldly declared the *10 Things I've Been Meaning To Say To Black*

*Women* at another open mic. The little girl that dared to dream had once again found her voice.

With time I grew stronger, and fear took a backseat to the faith that my parents raised me to have. Now each time I pick up a pen or step to a mic, I think about some of the people who got me to this point: My family (Michael and Darice Whitted, Kyle Whitted, Leila Whitted, Bernice Herron, Raymond and Michele Penn, Aretha Jones, and all of my extended family), those who trained me in song (Martrice Edge, Joan Reed, and Nancy Mirocha), those who taught me to dance (William and Rosalie Green), those who encouraged my spiritual development and creativity (Caroloretta Tucker, Kirsten Alley, Toni Pearson, and Bonnie Matthews), those who saw something in me and gave me a chance (Bernie Jablonski, Chuck Smith, Runako Jahi, and Mike Malone), those who pulled it out of me 'kicking and screaming' ("Mama" Brenda Matthews), all of the girls who have ever looked up to me (Ladies of Virtue, Junior Instruments of Praise, Victory Thunderettes, Anointed In Movement), and those that I looked up to (Victory Apostolic Church Family, The Ballet Centre Family). I think of so many people, even those who only sought to break me. They were with me on my journey to *Things I've Been Meaning To Say*, and they are with me still. They made me the woman I am.

And for this, I am thankful.

> Memories of you
> freely flow out of my heart
> every time I speak.

# When She Speaks

A collection of words and thoughts...Vol. 2

# The Soul Is Stirred

# Declarations

I'm tired of being silent.
I'm tired of silently watching
the ships of life go by
praying for mine to come in
and waiting for life to begin.
I'm tired of constantly apologizing
for taking up valuable space
and time
that can be used
by a worldly successful fool.
And I'm tired
of the self-inflicted pain
and the judgment received from you.
Somewhere along the line,
I forgot
that my price tag read priceless
and that my possibilities,
like art,
are endless in my God's eyes.
I began to value myself by
the length of my hair,
my shape,
my size,
my life station,
my education –
and I took my focus off the prize.
No longer can I despise myself
for the chains that I got bound in.
Chains are meant to be broken,
and I was made to win.
So with every ounce of strength

and faith within,
I make this declaration and I say,
"Give me what's mine."

Give me what's mine,
everything that's owed to me.
I'm walking forward
in boldness and authority.
Complacency is finished
and failure has bored me.
I'm taking back everything
that's been stolen from me.
Give me what's mine
or I'll take it by force.
I've made enough errors
and depression has run its course.
But I'm still standing.
I'm strong,
beautiful,
and proud.
My head is held high
and I'm living out loud.
I'm reclaiming my birthright,
everything that's owed to a queen –
my power
my purpose
my pleasure
my peace
my passion
my pedestal
and most importantly
my praise.
And yes,
I know I can't go back

and make up for lost days.
So,
I'll carry myself gently
like a Black Tie rose.
I'll move like a millionaire
in a room full of CEOs.
I'll shake hands with the rich,
extend alms to the poor,
and gladly give it away freely
since I know I'll get more.
I'm comfortable with what I am
and what I never will be.
I can't walk in your shoes;
I gotta do this for me.
Yes, my past has hurt me,
and many people have let me go.
But I still move forward,
because my God told me so.
And since He
Gives me direction,
Opens my eyes to revelation, and
Determines my destination,
I can still claim the victory
despite your "No."

And with my individualistic intellect
and my beauty divine,
I walk in not looking a thing
like what I've been through
and I do it in perfect time.

Am I cocky?
Maybe.
But I know where my faith lies.

With my posture erect
and my face toward the skies,
I let the Son shine on me
and guide my pathway.
So,
you can join me,
applaud me,
or get out of my way.

# Sista Solitude

Sometimes,
even the most social of sistas
need solitude.
We speak endlessly
about whatever comes to mind,
but we don't take the time
to listen and appreciate the silence.
We mentor selflessly
to anyone who calls our name,
but we don't focus on the One
who is trying to advise us.
We are wives,
mothers,
sisters,
daughters,
teachers,
students,
lovers of life,
and friends.
We are women,
born to give and extend.
We pour into others
without pause to replenish
our own soul.
So if I,
being one of those sistas,
would like to take a moment away,
I sincerely hope you do not
find it to be strange.

# A Recipe For Pound Cake

You said that I hooked you
with my sweetness.
It was Mama's tradition
passed down to me.
She said,
"Sweeten it with soul,
sift it with spirit,
then again for good measure
from the heart.
Add your wisdom slowly,
keeping it warm for consistency,
then blend it with skill and experience.
Make it special with your sass.
Purify it with a prayer.
Line your pan with passion
and fill with care.
Be patient as the fire
turns it into what it should be,
and be vigilant so that you
time it perfectly."
So shortcuts weren't an option,
at least not for me.
Homemade in the kitchen –
thick and sweet.
Maybe you were right.
I hooked you with my sweetness.
It was Mama's tradition
passed down to me.
But to tell you the truth,
I wouldn't have done it differently.

# Upon Admiration

Opening the door
to unknown possibility,
I search my mind for
reasons to exhibit reserve.
At this point,
what purpose would it serve?
Every day of my
so-called life,
I've played it safe
in two-inch water
and dived head first
into bottomless oceans.
Now I'm faced with an opportunity
to boldly go where
I have never gone before.
Still,
my feet shuffle backward
like a rhythmless six-year-old
in a professional conservatory.
I don't belong here
(so I've been told),
but this is the place
where fate has lead me.
My heart begs me,
"Sit this one out!"
My head
calculates all possible outcomes
for an ego too delicate to bruise.
Which way will I choose,
if only one route
is guaranteed not to lose?

Light at the end of the tunnel
beckons me to move forward.
With memory left to warn me,
I still push onward
into an unknown symphony of music,
movement,
and emotion –
leaving to chance
what the topic
of my next penned thought
will be.

# 'Nuff Said

I am
in my opinion
a chameleon.
I'll explain:

I'm always changing,
never predictable,
and able to be seen
live and in color
by anyone who wants
to get to know me.
I am the daughter of the moon,
seeing through the night
with ease.
I'm sensitive in spirit
yet strong in heart.
Giving my all
is not an option;
it's a requirement.
I'm maternal
outgoing
emotional
caring
and crazy!
When you want
an honest opinion,
I'll be the one to give it to you.
I'm a procrastinator
and a perfectionist.
And I'm me.
'Nuff said.

I'm a leader;
but sometimes,
I'd like to follow.
I can be shy
around those
that I don't know,
but warm and loving
once I am comfortable.
I'm tough yet soft.
Humble yet hard-headed.
And gorgeous!
Drop dead I might add!
I'm a woman.
I'm a Black woman.
And I'm me.
'Nuff said.

# Lady In Red

for Ntozake Shange

I feel your words,
Ntozake,
as they pierce
my spirit
with compassion
and conviction
for the plight
you put before me.
I can identify
with the women
and the rainbows
that they cross over.
And your words
give me courage
to move on
"without assistance",
to love God,
pull Him into myself,
and sing
and dance
my story.

# Love Is Evident

# Coffee Shop

I glanced up from my
mocha latte
while reading my favorite
Maya Angelou book
when I noticed him.
He was brown as the chocolate cookie
on which I had only taken
two bites.
Tall,
debonair,
beautiful and breathtaking.
I could tell from his stride
that he was about something.
I felt the soul of him,
his deep inner being
that exuded from his smile.
And I thought:
If I could get you to notice
the empty seat next to me,
then you could get a taste
of my intellect
and find out why I
am your destiny.
Yeah, I'd impress you.
You'd be feeling me
as much as I'm feeling you.
And we'd be feeling something.
Something real.
Something true.
Something ours.
Now wouldn't that feel good?
But as he grabbed his order,

not once looking in my direction,
I sat paralyzed.
I watched him exit my life
as quickly as he walked in.
My mouth won't speak
unless my heart says go.
And so,
I went back to my latte
and my Maya
as I chilled
in a coffee shop.

# Gentlemen

What happened to the day
when gentlemen walked the earth
proudly and freely?
Did they disappear?
Was I delusional
and they were never here?
I heard that there was a time
when a man would make social calls
before booty call hours.
He would show you a good time
without a word of sexual intent.
Someone told me that these men,
called gentlemen,
would open doors for you.
They would give you a coat
in cold weather
and treat you with respect.
Not because he had to
or as a means to an end,
but because he was born to.
He knew you were a lady;
you didn't have to remind him.
Where did they go?
Do they still exist?
I heard
that these gentlemen
would hold your hand,
listen,
and truly understand.
He made your heart
feel free to love,

and he knew the meaning
of the word no.
You never thought twice
of safety,
and the purity of his heart
made your spirit glow.
It's beautiful to know
that these gentlemen existed,
but I fear
that I may have missed
this golden era of men.
And if I am wrong,
please return again.

# I Wasn't Trying To Love You
it just sounded like something he/you would say


I didn't want to hurt you,
but I wasn't trying to love you either.
I enjoy your company,
but your closeness is not necessary.
I care but I can't commit
to a relationship beyond platonic.
And I'm sorry if this hurts you,
but I wasn't trying to love you.
I want you
but I don't need you
for more than what you are.
Honestly,
you never had all that I needed.
And I'm sure
that you are wondering
what purpose you serve —
as well you should.
Never doubt
that there are feelings here,
though not strong enough
to get me to leave.
My hands are tied.
Either way,
someone will lose.
And so I choose to stay.
Because after all,
I wasn't trying to love you.

# Daydreaming

Can't concentrate
only contemplate
the love you give to me.
I anticipate
and can hardly wait
for the day we come to be.
Can you relate
to my loving state?
Is it something only I see?
Or can you initiate
my hope for a loving fate
and turn my dream into reality?

# Symbiosis

He understands me.
Not the conventional me
or the masked identity
that I have perfected
for the world to see,
but the real, unadulterated me.
Without question,
he sees beauty in my
imperfections.
In my flawed reflection,
he sees perfect femininity.
Never planned on it.
Would have bet everything
against it.
Yet, here I am
feeling giddy like a schoolgirl
with her first crush.
He makes me feel like
even my lack is enough,
and I am strengthened
with his simplistic touch.
Some say
that this is love's true basis.
I agree.
But right now,
I am safely settled
in symbiosis.
We better each other
in mental and emotional doses.
As I pour into him,
he pours into me.

Collectively,
we move forward in a bond
untitled.
This relationship
flows through my veins.
When the world gets
too much for him,
I keep him sane.
When fear grips my heart,
he's the breath of courage
that pushes me on.
His eyes give me vision;
my smile keeps him strong.
Tell me,
could it be long
before worlds collide
in a way not intended?
I'd pull away,
but every part of me
you've mended
as I have healed you.
We have a bond
untainted by the world's views.
Simplistic,
honest,
and clothed in God's truth.
But isn't that what
a true friendship
is supposed to do?

# My Letter To Atlas

I see you
carrying the weight of the world
on your shoulders.
I know that weight is more
than a thousand boulders.
Your story has never been told –
mainly out of fear.
You don't know who to trust,
so let me make this clear.
I am here for your person
and not your persona.
Even when it is gone,
I will still be here for you.
Know that you're not alone.
As long as you have me,
your heart has a home.

I understand
that even the strongest man
gets weak.
The most eloquent orators
lose the words to speak.
And though it's peace that you seek,
you find your funds being depleted.
Just know that even when you lose,
you are never fully defeated.
You may think that you have
what you've always needed,
but I have what you lack.
I am the cure
to your Achilles' heel

and I will always have your back.
Take that for a fact,
no matter how far you roam.
As long as you have me,
your heart has a home.

And forgive me if I wasn't there
when you needed me.
You called my name,
but my past hurt and pain
kept me from responding unselfishly.
I was taught
to preserve myself first,
to stand on my own two feet,
and that putting my own ambition
aside to love
was considered foolish and weak.
I know now that loving you
does not make me less than I am.
Where I fall short,
you step in and support
all my dreams,
my goals,
and my plans.
Who knew that a man like you
could melt this heart of stone?
As long as you have me,
your heart has a home.

So please,
stop wasting your time
on people unworthy of you.
Your blessings don't come easy
and only real friends

understand that truth.
In fact,
your blessings come in
overalls and boots
and look a lot like work.
Often you find yourself
looking around for help
but left alone and hurt.
Lesson learned.
Your truth you've earned
while all others are hostile.
Words and thoughts
don't mean much
if what they are preaching
ain't gospel.
Self-appointed apostles
cannot possibly
knock you off of your throne.
As long as you have me,
your heart has a home.

# Her People Are United

# Cry

Let the women cry out.
We have lost enough sons
and the sun itself
is refusing to shine on our dark skin.
Our men are busy
fighting territorial wars
and trying to knock down doors
that God locked for a reason.
If there is to be peace in this season,
it is time
for the women to cry out.

Let the women cry out,
and maybe then
our brothers will hear us.
Have we lost all respect for ourselves?
Do we not see that
races no longer fear us?
Not the alpha male fear
that you've been preoccupied
in seeking,
but the respect for solid leading
and forward thinking.
The race is sinking,
so let the women cry out.

Let the women cry out,
or we don't stand a chance.
When will we understand
that it's not about
how many followers you have

or what you said that you did
or your silver tongue
or the gun you grip
or your street connection
or your fortune and fame
or your hustle
or your grind
or your success
or your name?
If you have no legacy,
you have only yourself to blame.
Truly enlightened minds
find time to seek the divine
and share with others.
You are nothing
without your brothers.
Yet,
you're so busy
pushing for power
and destroying your fellow man
that you refuse to understand
the need to foster unity.
So if there is to be
an end to this insanity,
it must be up to femininity.
Right?

Let the women cry out.
Enough.

# Jungles

No trees.
Just buildings
and leaves
of glass.

The sun doesn't shine here.
Trees of brick
shade the sun's light.
Metal rain and gun smoke
fill the air,
killing game –
young, strong Black men.
Duck!
Get low!
Rain makes you wet.
Be careful not to drown.
It's about survival.
Must steal to make ends meet
for the sake of the tribe,
naturally.

No trees.
Just buildings
and leaves
of glass.

Overpopulation
due to impregnation of young.
Still nursing on momma's milk
before being forced to fight
for the right to live.

No shame.
No power.
Nothing but faith
that this child will be different.
Named Imani,
hoping she'll be the one
to follow the star
out of the jungle
and guide her people
through the wild
and back home.

No trees.
Just buildings
and leaves
of glass.

No light.
No shelter.
No mercy.
Society watches
this National Geographic spin-off
as we are hunted,
persecuted,
and placed on display
for even past indiscretions
to be scrutinized as valid.
Nova can't touch
the pain that mothers feel
as their sons,
the future leaders of the pack,
are taken one by one.
Death in the hands
of cold metal rain.

Duck!
Get low!
Rain makes you wet.
Be careful not to drown.
Children of God,
born under the stipulation
that we are all just lost
in the jungle
and can never get out.

No trees.
Just buildings
and leaves
of glass.

# Black Mother's Plea

for our fallen sons – we speak your name

Times are different, my son.
Racial tensions
are high and
you are beautifully brown.
Very proud you should be, though
openly the world opposes your
now blossoming life.
True, we need to fight; or maybe
all we need is
more understanding.
I pray for change daily, while
readily those in power
wait for the quickest
availability to dim your
light.
Times are different, my son.
Each day, another prince
releases his last breath and another
mother mourns.
I weep with them,
crying tears and
holding hands in prayer for
all our sons and daughters.
Each time you
leave my sight,
every day I
release you to the world,
I pray for this one thing –
come home alive.

# The Call

for "Mama" Brenda Matthews

This is a call
to all of my people
who still believe
that we have purpose.
I am calling you
to stand and prove
that our race isn't the worthless
and tradable commodity
the world has labeled us to be.
I am calling
searching
seeking out those
who believe that sentences
are meant to be spoken
and not served.
Where are my people
who understand that education
is deeper than a right —
it's a necessity?
Where are those who
encourage knowledge,
support wisdom,
and foster understanding?
Lack of a ball or a beat
shouldn't determine your destiny,
and living off of borrowed money
ain't all it's cracked up to be.

This is a call
to all of my people

who still believe
in dignity and class.
Those who believe
that a woman's worth
is not all wrapped up in her
physical assets
but rather in her assessment of self.
Understand that you are a jewel
of immeasurable wealth.
Stop waiting on permission to live.
Abandon your fears
and follow your dreams.
Appreciate and honor your temple.
As good as he may seem,
only one is truly worthy
to enter your inner court.
We need to be each other's support,
soft enough to walk beside our men,
and strong enough
to hold them up if need be.
Ladies, check your history.
The strongest women
handled home and community
simultaneously.
Build up our brothas.
Remind them of their worth.
But never forget to care for yourself
first.

And where are my real, strong brothas?
Where are the kings
who once ruled kingdoms
with the love and wisdom
passed down from the ancestors?

I am calling to my brothas
who want better.
If there is no path,
make one.
Despite uncertainty in your chances,
take one.
You can fight your flaws
and wisely raise
your sons and daughters.
Own your thrown.
Stop leaving your queen alone
to raise what it took two to make.
You want respect?
We want the same.
Remember,
there is more at stake
than what is visible today.

This is a call
to all of my people
who believe that hope isn't lost.
Where are those
who can stand for the fallen
left lying in the streets?
Who will pick up the battles
not yet won?
At one point,
we walked arm-in-arm as one.
Now,
petty arguments are probable cause
to end life with a gun.
Where are my sistas?
Where are my brothas?
The time has come

where we can no longer afford to be
voluntarily misled
or complacently silent.

So this is a call
to the sons of Martin,
Malcolm,
Marcus,
and Medgar.
The daughters of Sojourner,
Harriet,
Rosa,
and Nikki.
Those who understand
that those four little girls
could be your children.
Those who know
that whistling and swinging still coincide.
Those who still have pride
in their melanin-kissed skin,
loving that it has been
purposely blessed by God.
Don't find it odd
that I am calling for you.
This renaissance is long overdue,
and it starts
with the few willing to do
what no one wants us to.
And that includes you.

This is a call
to all of my people
who still believe
that

our
lives
matter
and we can thrive.
I'm calling you.
He's calling you.
Rise.

# Being Black

Being Black
does not mean
that you must sacrifice your pride
to make it in a world
that said you couldn't
from the start.
Being Black
does not mean
that you must settle for the norm
instead of creating the new.
Being Black
does not mean
that you are born a failure,
destined to lose,
and doomed to die
without purpose realized.
Being Black
does not mean that you
look down on your people

who do not have your blessings
or have achieved your status –
because we all jump the same hurdles.
But to be Black,
to be really Black,
means that you push,
you pull,
and you pursue
until the common goal is attained.
That is Black.

# Celebration Of Brown

Shades of brown sugar –
sweet to the taste.
Sons and daughters of the diaspora,
connected despite being misplaced.
Told by many
that our melanin is a sin,
though many spend millions
to darken tone
and fill bodies with collagen
to emulate what we received
due to our origin.
So as before, I will again
celebrate my beautiful brown.

Shades of chocolate –
soulful in its hues.
I'm celebrating the natural sway
of our native song.
The gospel truth of our
rhythm and blues
beats echoes of lands
that our eyes have never seen.
Bloodlines tied to royalty
while using lyricist's bars to
spit the psalms of the streets
that we now rule.
Whether institution or intuition,
still no fool.
So I chose
to celebrate my beautiful brown.

Shades of ebony –
not a novelty or choice.
We're willing to wear the color
when the weight is hard to bear
or there's an attempt
to mute the voice.
We live this.
Daily, we bleed red,
breathe black,
and pursue the green light
of the goals laid before us.
We are favored and covered
by the prayers of our ancestors.
We will not apologize
for our ambition to strive for better.
Instead, we will together
celebrate our beautiful brown.

Shades of black –
negro, preto, or noir.
A culture constantly evolving,
leaving behind legacies of
resilience and strength.
Knowledge spilling from
a head of thick coils –
cut low, straightened,
or intact as an afro.
We grow
stronger despite opposition
and wiser without permission.
This is the legacy
that we leave
to the next generation.

Our lives are cause
for genuine celebration.
So celebrate our beautiful brown.

# The Truth Is Heard

# White Girl

People tell me
that I'm a white girl
trapped inside a Black girl's body.
I'm a nappy head
without a conscious mind
or a miseducated hottie
(but only when dressed properly).
Because I'm suburban,
I can't claim to be African American.
But maybe there's somebody out there
like me
who can understand.

I think it's because
I choose to use proper grammar.
Since I have the choice
between Ebonics and English,
I will always choose the latter.
And when I walk into an interview,
I want them to see me –
not the negative stereotypes
that tend to precede me.
Or maybe it's because
I praise education and free speech.
I understand
that when I learn something,
I now have an obligation to teach.
I honor educators over athletes
and intellect over lies.
Those with that
crabs-in-a-barrel mentality
I tend to despise.

Or maybe that's just the view
from my eyes?

But what do I know?

'Cuz I'm just a white girl
trapped inside a Black girl's body.
I'm a nappy head
without a conscious mind
or a miseducated hottie
(but only when dressed properly).
Because I'm suburban,
I can't claim to be African American.
But maybe there's somebody out there
like me
who can understand.

Maybe it's because
I don't have six different kids
by five different baby daddies.
Plagued with uncertainty about paternity
while trying to prove who's the pappy.
And I don't worry
about getting my check on time;
because when I do give birth,
my husband will be by my side.

Or is that only how it works in my mind?

Or maybe,
just maybe,
it's because I don't have enough…
I'm the kind of sista
that brothas tend to let pass.

I operate out of class
and the common sense inside of me.
I don't want you to see my thong;
I would rather you know my theology.
Or before you get with me physically,
learn the real me intimately.
Over coffee,
we can discuss Christ,
scriptures,
and poetry.
Or maybe before you lay with me,
you should put a ring on it and marry me.
'Cuz I'm not talking temporarily;
I'm a woman designed for eternity.

Or do Black folk still get married?

But what do I know?

'Cuz I'm just a white girl
trapped inside a Black girl's body.
I'm a nappy head
without a conscious mind
or a miseducated hottie
(but only when dressed properly).
Because I'm suburban,
I can't claim to be African American.
But maybe there's somebody out there
like me
who can understand.

# Bitter, Party Of One

I guess I can't get mad.
It's not like
I didn't know of
or condone your nature.

The truth is
I thought that I could change you.
The good times were few,
but that small taste of sweet
made the sour bearable.

And that was my fault.

So when I see you with her,
I can't get mad.
All I can do is pull up a chair
and stomach the foolishness
that I allowed to stay on my plate.

I hear the humble pie is good here.

# A Eulogy For Beauty

She was beautiful once.
Skin cocoa-kissed by the sun,
flawless and smooth
with amber hues.
A proud woman of morals and virtue,
a rare and real jewel.
Her natural crown was short and full,
her smile was vibrant,
and her almond brown eyes
radiated a warmth
that beamed from the soul itself.
An educated woman,
she didn't rely on anyone else
to carry her load.
In fact,
she was the backbone of her family –
carrying the bloodline out of necessity
and doing it with grace and style.
Only woman in her family
to graduate high school and college,
serve her country,
and still keep a demeanor
that was godly and mild.
Any mother would be grateful
to claim her as their child.

Then, she met him –
a package presented perfectly
that seemed to compliment
her femininity.
He gave her willingly

the things her heart desired
but her hands couldn't obtain.
Love,
or so it was called by name.
Stated early in order to get the prize
between her thighs,
she freely gave
and didn't think twice of the same.
Beauty didn't know
that this was all an elaborate game.
And he showed no shame
as the fountain of interest
started to drain.

She was beautiful once.
Now the light in her eyes
is starting to dim.
What was once reciprocity
turned into a reality cold and grim.
He took advantage of her
unconditional love
without contemplating the effect on her.
He turned her house into his.
He used her check
to pay his child support
but made her abort both of their kids.
Profanity replaced praises
and fidelity was replaced by his fist.
His only reply:
"It is what it is."

So I cry for her.
I intercede for her.
I pray that she'll look at herself

and remember the woman
that she used to be –
one who appreciated her uniqueness
and did not place her destiny
on hold for a man
that was not meant to be.
Now, that flawless cocoa skin
is housing bruises
internally and externally.
The sad part is
that she thinks we can't see.
Her vibrant spirit is worn and defeated.
She has allowed Beauty to die
and accepted her new name –
Beaten.

She was beautiful once,
but all I can do is hope
that the scales are removed
from her eyes
so she can see that
this
is
not
love.
Each day, she dies spiritually.
In her situation,
physical is eminent
unless she remembers and reclaims
who she truly is again.

# Letter 628
my final thoughts on the matter

For the record,
I never questioned our friendship.
To the inconsistency, I remained blinded.
You struggle, I struggle.
I struggle…
you're nowhere to be found.
You were emotionally divested and intangible,
leaving me feeling unmanageable.
'Some kind of way', they say.

For the record,
I never asked for more
than I was willing to give.
I never claimed to mirror perfection;
reciprocity is how I chose to live.
I learned that bonds break
when the inner ear is tuned to those outside.
Maybe we could've mended the tear
had it not been for your pride.

And for the record,
I never sought self-preservation
in a bond pledged to be selfless.
My mistake was granting unmerited trust.
So, I stepped away selfishly
to find the peace that was meant to be.
Removed were those not a part of my destiny.
And frankly, that's fine with me.
It took separation to see the truth
that it's different when it comes to you.

# 10 Things I've Been Meaning To Say To Black Women

because sistas, you've been on my mind…

Ten…
If you are comfortable
with being called a 'dyme',
allow me to inform you
that you are being short-changed.
You were created
by an Omnipotent Being
to have infinite possibilities
that cannot be counted on a man's hand.
Own it.
Believe that who you are created to be
cannot be classified by a number.

Nine…
You may have a cat,
but you are not one.
YOLO will leave you solo
after the night of fun is done.
And since illness and impregnation
cannot be undone,
I suggest that you live
your one life wisely.

Eight…
You are what you eat,
and sadly most of us have neglected
to give our temple
its regularly scheduled maintenance.
Your raggedness is starting to show.

Stress, sadness, or genetic disposition
can no longer be used
as the excuse or permission
for what we have done
to ourselves.

Seven…
times seventy is the number
of times that we are to forgive.
Your days of being a bitter black woman
will continue until you learn to let it go.
Yes, he hurt you.
Yes, you were unfairly passed up.
But if you keep pouring negativity
into your soul's cup,
it will kill you.
Then who will be left to handle your load?

Six…
We accept this
as the number of imperfection,
but we can't accept the reflection
that God placed in the mirror.
We pay to change
what God has already ordained,
hoping that we can see clearer.
Looking at yourself through the
eyes of another
will only leave you blind.
When you were created,
you were made correctly
the first time.

Five...
Spiritual
Physical
Emotional
Sexual
Mental.
All elements of your being
that must be developed and nourished
in God's Kairos time.
It is only when these elements
are properly aligned
that you will truly know
what you are placed here...

Four...
God so loved the world
that He gave His Son
as a sacrifice for you.
That is perfect love
that is waiting for you to
simply accept it.
Love from the Father
builds love for yourself
and that's a love that you'll never regret.

Three...
Despite what the media tells you,
there is not
(I repeat, NOT)
a shortage of good men in this world.
Why are you allowing yourself
to be used as a third wheel?
I understand that you love him,
and have needs

that you think he can fulfill.
But once he's scratched that itch,
you are quickly dismissed.
And why would you want someone
who doesn't belong to you?
If you can take him from her,
someone can take him from you…

Two…
There are two things in life
that are consistent –
God and change.
We pray for serenity,
then we go crazy
over things that are outside of our control.
Why not lighten the load
and place those things
into the hands of One who won't…

One…
You are beautiful.
You are unique.
You are the treasure
that ultimately every man seeks.
There is fire in the depths of your belly
and it manifests
every time that you speak.
So speak up!
Stand up!
You have a race to run.
Keep running your race
until God calls you home
and says, "Well done."

# Beauty's Sonnet

I found my beauty immeasurable –
a search that I have spent my life to find.
T'was a longing through fear most terrible
in the dark depths of the heart, soul, and mind.
Was not in the opinion of masses,
nor was it bought with money at high price.
Couldn't find it in high or low passes,
nor in solemn or in foolish advice.
But what I longed for always was within,
though patiently dormant she did reside.
Quietly, she pleaded just to begin
until her simple cries I could not hide.
        Now at this moment, I stand proud and free
        while celebrating my own true beauty.

# Her God Listens

# One Day At A Time

I won't ask
for You to move every mountain
the moment
I lift my hands in prayer.
I can't ask
for You to avenge every pain
that I endure
at the hands of others.
It would be unfair to me
to make all my ways easier,
all of my burdens lighter,
and all of my worries disappear.
For I know
these trials are necessary
and controlled by You
to mold me into
a woman of substance.
So all I ask
is that one day at a time,
You give me the grace,
peace,
mercy,
and strength
to make it to the next time
I pray.

# My Desire
a spiritual request

Hide me in Your Heart, Lord.
I have nowhere else to run.
Keep me in Your Loving Arms
'til the setting of the sun.

Hold me in Your Hands, Lord,
so that I won't be plucked out.
Lift my head so that I can be
free from fear and doubt.

Help me do Your Will, Lord.
I want to do things right.
It's Your Word that I follow in the day
and meditate on at night.

Hear me when I call, Lord.
I'm calling out to You
to give me grace, to guide my way,
and fulfill what You've asked me to do.

# The Weight

Lay down the stress of the world.
The need to carry it all
doesn't apply here.
Relax into me
as I breathe life into you,
cast out your fear and doubt,
and minister to you
by simply holding you in my arms.
I wish that I could
keep you safe from all harm,
but my human limitations fail me.
Let me be
that one that stands by you
in the storm.
The rains will come,
as it is His Will;
still, I'll hold your hand
and we'll push through together.
Tell me your darkest secrets
and I will find the light in them.
Show me the scars
on your body and heart
and I will lay hands on them,
pray for them,
and heal them.
And when the pain is too much
and the wound is too deep,
let me embrace you
until you fall asleep.
Show me your tears.
Release the anger and resentment

that you have held through the years.
I will sit right here and listen.
You've never had someone
that you could bare your all to,
but I have been commissioned
to be what you've been missing –
a friend without condition.
I don't care where you've been,
who you've hurt,
or who has hurt you.
All that matters is
the weight that you carry
is too much for you.
I want nothing more for you
than to release it,
place it in God's Hands,
pray for Him to decrease it,
then wait for His reply
and be at peace with it.
And while you seek the face of God,
I will stand in the gap for you.
I will intercede for you,
plead for you,
and tell wars to cease for you.
Not because you asked me to,
but because you need me to.
Everyone needs someone sometimes.
I have been sent to be your blessing
during this storm of life.
Lay down the stress of the world.
The need to carry it all
doesn't apply here.
Relax into me
as I breathe life into you,

cast out your fear and doubt,
and minister to you
by simply holding you in my arms.
And when morning comes,
I will carry the weight with you.

# Every Word Spoken

Every word spoken
becomes a mountain moved,
a wall left crumbled,
and the sands of time dispelled.
Every word spoken
becomes a river started
and a spirit once
brokenhearted
is mended as quickly as it fell.
Every word spoken
summons the Father's Light,
sends demons to flight,
and makes everything unclear
as certain as the day.
Every word spoken
restores sight to the blind,
corrects errors in time,
and fills the darkness
with bright sunrays.
Every word spoken
chips away at every doubt,
reveals what beauty is about,
and makes perfection
seem pale in comparison to
what is right.
Every word spoken
makes worries seem small,
makes the weakest stand tall
and strong enough to fight.

# God's Creation

Our lives are like the creation:

God must first prepare us.
He shows us the light.
He separates the concrete
from the unnecessary.
He creates the ground
for us to stand on.

Then He opens His mouth
to speak into existence
the situations and circumstances
in which we will dwell.
Each item is formed
to make us what we should be
in order to fulfill our purpose.

Finally, He forms us.
He takes delight and care
in personally touching
the pinnacle of His Creation.
Not spoken into existence,
but made by hand
with intent and love.
And when He sees us,
a complete masterpiece,
He will say,
"It is very good."

# Nothing

Is there a war too hard to fight?
Is there a time too dark of night?
Is there a matter too deeply involved?
Is there a problem without resolve?
Is there a door that's locked and closed?
Is there an answer that He doesn't know?
Not one
Not at all.
Nothing.

Is there a house to torn to build?
Is there a life to worn to live?
Is there a road too hard to cross?
Is there a battle already lost?
Is there a child too wrong to save?
Is there a prayer too hard to pray?
Not one
Not at all.
Nothing.

He is the Almighty God.
For Him, there is nothing too hard.
We may get weary of being still,
but time and space moves at His Will.
Is there a time our faith should concede?
Is there a time He can't meet your need?
Not one
Not at all.
Nothing.

# What More Can I Do?
an epilogue

I wish I was just a little richer,
had the money of many in my hand.
I could provide for my brothers and sisters.
I could change the lack of man.
I wish I had the powers of a healer.
With one touch, I'd cure ache and disease.
I'd give a smile that mends and eases,
or offer an embrace to set the captive free.
But in all my hope, I'm just one person.
I'm limited to what to share with you.
So with my heart and soul,
I bow to God in prayer and cry,
"What more can I do?"

I wish that I was wise to teach the masses,
to give lessons on how to write and read.
I'd educate all the world's children,
regardless of status or creed.
I wish I could show the world what love is;
maybe then we'd love our fellow man.
I'd lead heart to hearts with those who've vowed to hate.
I'd breathe life so everyone could stand.
But in all my hope, I'm just one person.
And though everything I wish is true,
I can only bow in prayer
with tears and heavy heart and cry,
"What more can I do?"

I wish that I can change the way that I used to think
before I knew what mattered most.
Maybe I could've made a difference

with the path that I would've chose.
But growing older makes you wiser,
and I know now what I couldn't see.
The world won't change unless you make it.
It all starts with you and me.
So take the hope of just one person,
let it echo through and through.
Please bow to God in prayer
with tears and heavy heart and cry,
"What more can I do?"

The fate of many
must first start with you.
So,
what more can you do?

www.ingramcontent.com/pod-product-compliance
Lightning Source LLC
Chambersburg PA
CBHW051705090426
42736CB00013B/2541